ARMADILLOS

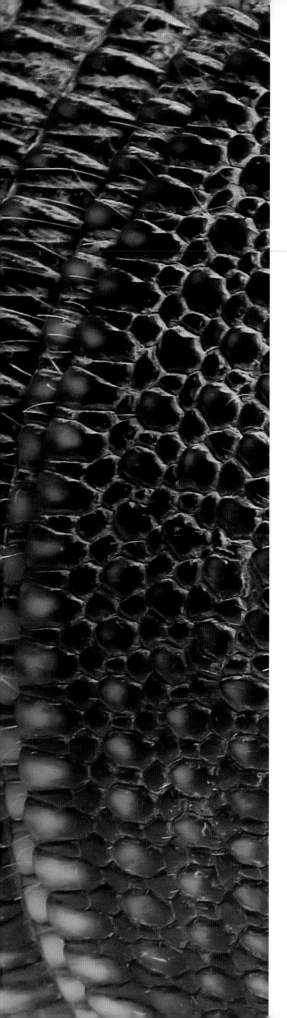

LIVING WILD

Published by Creative Education and Creative Paperbacks
P.O. Box 227, Mankato, Minnesota 56002
Creative Education and Creative Paperbacks are imprints of The Creative Company
www.thecreativecompany.us

Design and production by Mary Herrmann
Art direction by Rita Marshall
Printed in China

Photographs by Alamy (Leonid Plotkin), Corbis (MARIO LOPEZ, Kevin Schafer),
Creative Commons Wikimedia (Anonymous/Colima, Arnaud boucher, Rusty Clark,
Daderot, DoxTxobv, Exlibris–commonswiki, Joseph M. Gleeson, Hazmat2, Kolossos, Vlad
Lazarenko, Ltshears, Mokkie, Pattycarabelli, pipeafcr, Prissantenbär, Guido Valverde, John
Woohouse Aubudon, Zuarin), Dreamstime (Lukas Blazek, Catalinr, Dekanaryas, Svetlana
Foote, Lukslukys), Getty Images (Pete Oxford), iStockphoto (Sloot), Shutterstock (belizar,
Maria Gaellman, guentermanaus, Arto Hakola, Irmairma, Andrea Izzotti, Heiko Kiera,
lalito, MyImages – Micha, Dr. Morley Read, Antonio Scorza, Brandon Seidel, zixian)

Library of Congress Cataloging-in-Publication Data
Gish, Melissa.
Armadillos / Melissa Gish.
p. cm. — (Living wild)
Includes bibliographical references and index.
Summary: A look at armadillos, including their habitats, physical characteristics such as their
armored bodies, behaviors, relationships with humans, and the threatened status of some
species in the world today.

ISBN 978-1-60818-703-4 (hardcover)
ISBN 978-1-62832-299-6 (pbk)
ISBN 978-1-56660-739-1 (eBook)
1. Armadillos—Juvenile literature. I. Title. II. Series: Living wild.

QL737.E23G57 2016
599.3'12—dc23   2015026813

CCSS: RI.5.1, 2, 3, 8; RST.6-8.1, 2, 5, 6, 8; RH.6-8.3, 4, 5, 6, 7, 8

First Edition HC 9 8 7 6 5 4 3 2 1
First Edition PBK 9 8 7 6 5 4 3 2 1

CREATIVE EDUCATION • CREATIVE PAPERBACKS

ARMADILLOS

Melissa Gish

Moonlight filters through the Colombian rainforest as a giant armadillo

curiously approaches a termite mound.

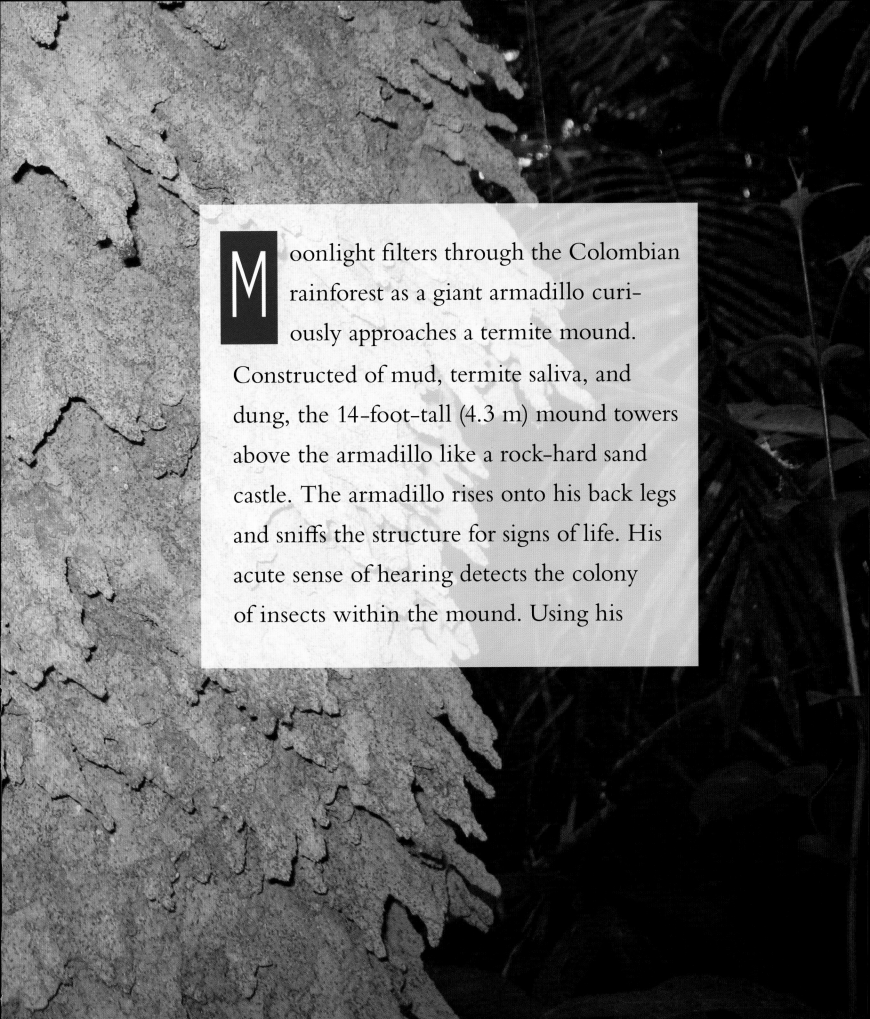

M oonlight filters through the Colombian rainforest as a giant armadillo curiously approaches a termite mound. Constructed of mud, termite saliva, and dung, the 14-foot-tall (4.3 m) mound towers above the armadillo like a rock-hard sand castle. The armadillo rises onto his back legs and sniffs the structure for signs of life. His acute sense of hearing detects the colony of insects within the mound. Using his

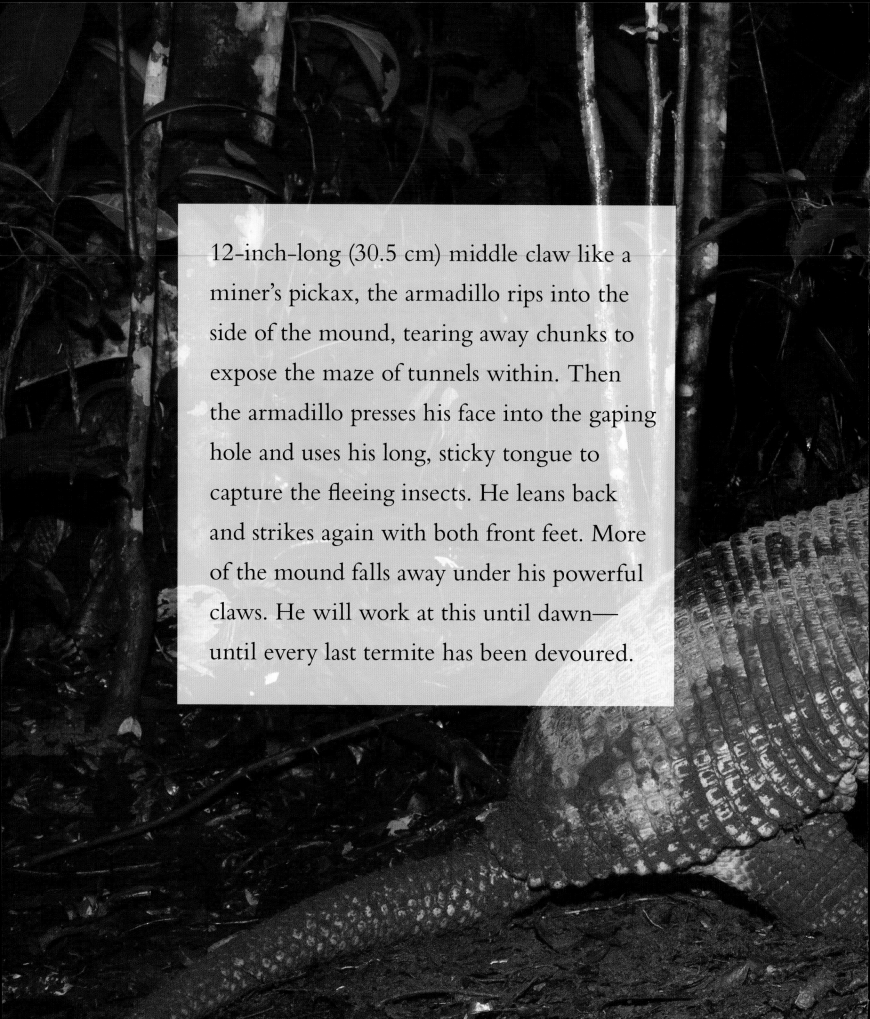

12-inch-long (30.5 cm) middle claw like a miner's pickax, the armadillo rips into the side of the mound, tearing away chunks to expose the maze of tunnels within. Then the armadillo presses his face into the gaping hole and uses his long, sticky tongue to capture the fleeing insects. He leans back and strikes again with both front feet. More of the mound falls away under his powerful claws. He will work at this until dawn— until every last termite has been devoured.

WHERE IN THE WORLD THEY LIVE

■ **Large Hairy Armadillo**
South America
(mainly Argentina)

■ **Pink Fairy Armadillo**
central Argentina

■ **Giant Armadillo**
northern half of
South America

■ **Southern Long-nosed Armadillo**
southern half of
South America

■ **Nine-banded Armadillo**
southern U.S.
through South
America

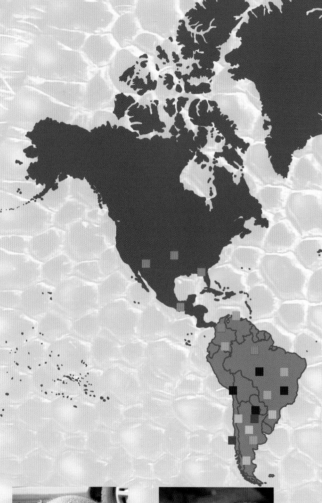

■ **Dwarf Armadillo (Pichi)**
Argentina, Chile

■ **Southern Three-banded Armadillo**
central regions of
South America

The 21 armadillo species are found throughout South America, with 1, the nine-banded armadillo, also present in North America. Some species are more common and wide-ranging than others, but all armadillos are elusive and solitary creatures. The colored squares represent typical locations of seven of the species living in the wild today.

With their armored bodies, armadillos are some of the most distinctive **mammals** in the animal kingdom. Armadillos and their closest relatives, anteaters and sloths, are classified in the superorder Xenarthra (*zee-NARTH-ra*), meaning "strange joints." Xenarthrans have extra joints in their necks and backs. Armadillos are the only members of the order Cingulata and the family Dasypodidae, named for a Latin phrase meaning "shaggy feet." The name "armadillo" is a 16th-century Spanish word that was pronounced *AR-ma-DEE-oh* and meant "little armored one." The Aztecs of ancient Mexico called armadillos *azotochtli*, or "turtle-rabbit."

All 21 species of armadillos are native to South America. Some species, such as the greater long-nosed and giant armadillos, range across the northern half of the continent. Other species, such as the large hairy, southern long-nosed, and greater fairy armadillos, inhabit the southern half of the continent. A few species have limited ranges. The pink fairy armadillo is found only in central Argentina, and the Yunga's lesser long-nosed armadillo lives only in northwestern Argentina. The

The armadillo is naturally immune to the **venom** of fire ants and can consume these insects without injury.

The naked-tailed armadillo species have thinner plates of armor than their relatives do.

Brazilian three-banded armadillo inhabits northeastern Brazil, and the hairy long-nosed armadillo is limited to the southwestern Andes of Peru. One species is familiar in North America. Native to Uruguay and northern Argentina, the nine-banded armadillo began moving north about 150 years ago. This species is now common in Mexico and the southern United States. Only one other species can be found outside South America. The northern naked-tailed armadillo inhabits upland plateaus from the southern tip of Mexico to Venezuela.

Glyptodonts, armadillo relatives that became **extinct** about 12,000 years ago, were about the size of a small car. Modern armadillos are not nearly as large as their ancestors. The giant armadillo is the largest species living today. It typically grows to about 3 feet (0.9 m) long and has an additional 20 inches' (50.8 cm) worth of tail. Its weight varies from 70 to 110 pounds (31.8–49.9 kg), depending on how much food is available. All other armadillo species are much smaller. The nine-banded can tip the scales at 17 pounds (7.7 kg), and the greater naked-tailed may weigh as much as 13 pounds (5.9 kg). Most other armadillos average 3 to 11 pounds (1.4–5 kg). The

Of the almost 500 different foods eaten by nine-banded armadillos, animals make up 90 percent.

The pichi takes frequent naps while foraging, lowering its body temperature by as much as 20 degrees.

dwarf armadillo, better known as the pichi in its native Argentina and Chile, weighs just two pounds (0.9 kg), but the greater fairy and pink fairy are the smallest armadillos. Just four to six inches (10.2–15.2 cm) long, these unusual species rarely weigh more than five ounces (142 g).

Armadillos are nocturnal animals, meaning they are most active at night. Unlike other nocturnal mammals, armadillos' eyes do not exhibit eyeshine, the reflection of light shined on the animals' eyes. Armadillos have poor eyesight, so they rely on sharp hearing and a keen sense of smell to detect prey, which is often hidden underground or in rotting trees and vegetation. Armadillos have short, strong legs with sharp, clawed toes used for digging. The hind feet have five toes. In some species, such as the Brazilian three-banded armadillo, the three middle toes are fused together, forming hoof-like claws. Depending on the species, the front feet have three to five toes. The front middle toe is longer than the others. It is used like a pickax to destroy rocky termite mounds, rip the bark from fallen trees, and tear into the burrows of spiders, scorpions, and other invertebrates.

Armadillos do not have true teeth. Rather, they possess molariform (molar-like) teeth along their cheeks. These peg-

Because of its spinal structure, the pink fairy armadillo cannot lift its tail.

The pink fairy armadillo can burrow so quickly that it can completely bury itself within seconds of being threatened.

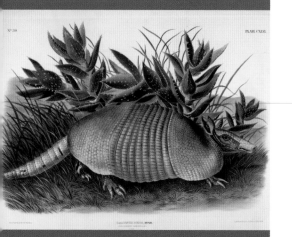

The armadillo was included in John J. Audubon's 1854 book, The Quadrupeds of North America.

shaped teeth lack the curves, dips, and hard enamel of true molars. Lost and regrown throughout an armadillo's life, molariform teeth are ideal for eating soft invertebrate prey. Most armadillos have 32 to 38 of these molar-like teeth. The exception is the giant armadillo; it possesses 80 to 100 teeth at any given time—the most of any mammal species.

The armadillo's most striking feature is its armor. Called a carapace, it is made of bone covered with about 2,000 tough, tiny scales called scutes. The scutes are made of keratin—the same substance that composes human fingernails. The carapace is divided into two parts: the anterior scapular shield, which covers the front of the armadillo's body, and the posterior pelvic shield, which covers the hindquarters. In the middle of the armadillo's body is a series of bands connected to each other by flexible tissue. The number of bands varies by species. Able to stretch and bend like an accordion, the bands give the armadillo flexibility. Some armadillo species have armored tails, while others do not. Tails are typically shorter than bodies. Armadillos have fur on their underbellies, but fur elsewhere depends on the species. The screaming hairy armadillo has scant bunches of long, coarse hairs jutting

Six-banded armadillos stay in the same burrows for longer periods of time than any of their relatives.

When curled up, a three-banded armadillo can roll even tighter to pinch a predator's nose or paw.

out from around its legs, while fairy armadillos have short, soft fur everywhere but their carapaces.

Contrary to popular belief, most armadillos cannot roll themselves into a ball. Only the southern and Brazilian three-banded armadillos are capable of this. (The Brazilian species was believed extinct until it was rediscovered in 1988 by Brazilian biologist Dr. José Maria Cardoso da Silva.) Because their carapaces are not attached to the skin on the sides of their bodies, they can tuck their limbs under their protective shells when threatened. Most predators then give up their attack.

For other armadillos, the best defense is running and hiding. While a few predators, such as jaguars and bears, can crush an armadillo's carapace, other armadillo enemies try to get the armadillo on its back to expose the soft underbelly. Though their claws can be used for defense, armadillos are slow-moving creatures and don't fight back very well. Instead, they try to startle a predator by jumping three to four feet (0.9–1.2 m) straight into the air. This typically makes escape possible. The carapace protects the armadillo from injury when it scuttles under a thorny bush or dives into a rocky shelter.

Armadillo burrows provide shelter for many other animals within the armadillo's ecosystem.

An armadillo will follow its keen sense of smell wherever it leads—even into impossibly tight places.

A VERY SHELL-TERED LIFE

While nine-banded armadillos have become a common sight across much of the southern U.S., armadillos in their native lands are some of the most elusive creatures in the world. They spend most of their time in underground burrows, emerging at night to forage. The slightest disturbance sends them immediately back underground—sometimes for the entire night. Until 2013, when a Brazilian research team set up motion-activated cameras, no one had ever seen a baby giant armadillo. Mariella Superina, a conservation biologist in Argentina, has been studying the pink fairy armadillo since 2000 but has *never* seen one of these creatures in the wild. So little is known about some armadillo species that the International Union for Conservation of Nature (IUCN) has listed them as data deficient, meaning it cannot determine if they are endangered or not. Armadillos are such **solitary** creatures that they rarely even associate with each other.

Each adult armadillo lives in a particular area called a home range. The size of an armadillo's home range varies by species. The largest species, the giant armadillo, has the

The three species of hairy armadillo are nocturnal in summer to avoid the heat but are diurnal in winter.

largest home range, typically between 1.7 and 3.8 square miles (4.4–9.8 sq km). The Brazilian three-banded armadillo has a home range of 0.5 to 0.9 square mile (1.3–2.3 sq km). Little is known about some species that suffer from habitat **fragmentation** due to human activity. Armadillos are powerful burrowers. To aid escape, armadillos will dig numerous burrows within their home range. Because armadillo populations are dense in many areas, their home ranges overlap. Rather than fight over territory, armadillos simply avoid one another for most of the year.

The exception to this solitary lifestyle comes during mating season, which lasts for about two months in late fall. Most armadillos' mating behaviors remain a mystery to scientists. Armadillos are old enough to mate by the time they reach 9 to 12 months. Male and female armadillos will mate with each other if their home ranges overlap, which means they typically have a number of partners. This is called polygamy. A pair of armadillos will spend several days together in a shared burrow, mating and feeding, before going their separate ways.

Hairy armadillos give birth twice a year, while other armadillo species give birth once a year. One

to three babies, called pups, develop from individual eggs. Uniquely, nine-banded armadillos give birth to quadruplets, or four offspring, from a single egg. The egg develops and splits into four separate **embryos** that are **genetically** identical to one another (known as natural clones). In unusual cases, the nine-banded armadillo will have three or five pups instead.

The normal **gestation** period for armadillos varies from 60 to 120 days. Like many other small mammals (such as skunks, raccoons, and badgers), armadillos may put the embryos' development "on hold." During this period, called embryonic diapause, the female armadillo's fertilized eggs turn into pinhead-sized balls of cells

Armadillos try to dig their burrows into hillsides as protection from pooling or streaming rainwater.

Like six-banded armadillos, pichis have carapaces that may be light yellow to tan.

that float in her **uterus** for a time before continuing to develop. Armadillos typically delay the progress of their embryos for three to four months, though periods of two years have been recorded. This period of delay is generally in response to environmental conditions. If pregnancy occurs late in the mating season, the pups will be born in winter, when food may be scarce. Delaying the process by a few months will enable the pups to be born during warmer weather and thus have a better chance of survival. Most armadillo pups are born between February and July.

Before giving birth, the female armadillo prepares a special burrow. She selects an isolated spot under dense, thorny brush or near rock piles or tree stumps. The tunnel may be up to 15 feet (4.6 m) in length, depending on the species, and is typically no wider than is necessary for the armadillo to crawl inside. She digs a chamber at the end of the tunnel. The chamber may be as wide as six feet (1.8 m) across. In this chamber, the female gives birth.

Newborn characteristics vary by species. Some newborn pups are miniature versions of their parents. Such species include nine-banded armadillos, which are

Baby armadillos do not develop fur like their parents' until they begin to mature.

Hairy armadillo species can have as many as 18 bands across their armored carapace.

The Andean hairy armadillo is known to kill snakes by jumping on them, slicing through the snakes with its sharp carapace.

born with their eyes open and can walk within a few hours. They are roughly the size of a stick of butter, weighing about four ounces (113 g). Other species are not fully developed at birth. For example, newborn three-banded armadillos' eyes remain closed, and they are deaf for the first three to four weeks. They are about the size of a golf ball and can roll into tight balls. The shells of all newborn armadillos are soft. Some species' shells harden within a few days, while others take a few weeks.

For several weeks (and sometimes longer, depending on the species), the pups are vulnerable and remain hidden inside the burrow, feeding on their mother's milk. In most armadillo species, month-old pups begin to venture outside with their mother, never straying far from the safety of the burrow. As they get older and braver, their mother takes them farther away from the burrow. If the security of the burrow is threatened, the mother may carry her offspring to a different burrow. Some species are **weaned** within two to three months, but others are not fully weaned until they reach four or five months old. Then they leave their mother to establish their own home ranges.

Once grown, the giant armadillo has few natural enemies. Smaller species, however, may fall prey to animals such as jaguars, whose bite can crush an armadillo shell. Anacondas can suffocate and swallow an armadillo whole. Harpy eagles may use razor-sharp talons to rip into an armadillo's soft underbelly. In North America, the leading predator of the nine-banded armadillo is the cougar. Black bears, coyotes, bobcats, and alligators also regularly feed on armadillos. Life span varies among armadillo species. The pichi typically lives about 9 years, while the six-banded armadillo can live 18 years. The large hairy armadillo may live 23 years. Some species do well in captivity, while others do not. Scotland's Edinburgh Zoo successfully bred southern three-banded armadillos in 2014, but pink fairy armadillos rarely survive more than a few weeks in captivity.

The Wildlife Center of Texas found that shots of vitamin C can save baby armadillos that are struggling to survive.

The Clyde Auditorium in Glasgow, Scotland, is nicknamed "The Armadillo" for its distinctive shape.

COOKIN' UP A LITTLE 'DILLO

B ecause armadillos are such secretive animals, most people have a limited view of these extraordinary creatures. In North America, the nine-banded armadillo has traditionally been considered a clumsy, lumbering animal without sense enough to stay off the highways. It has earned the nickname "Texas speed bump" because it so often ends up as **roadkill**. In South America, the pink fairy armadillo is nicknamed "sand swimmer" for its speedy, effortless burrowing, but most other armadillo species are simply considered dinner. Armadillos have been a valuable food source in their native lands for thousands of years.

In 2013, Romina Frontini and Rodrigo Vecchi, two scientists studying ancient cultures in Argentina, discovered the charred remains of armadillo shells among pottery and other artifacts at an **archaeological** site roughly 9,000 years old. Since modern people in Argentina cook armadillos in the shell, the scientists wondered if this practice has been passed down through the generations. They conducted an experiment, cooking six armadillos with fire and hot coals as early humans would have done. The remains of

With 74 percent protein and just 26 percent fat, armadillo meat is similar in content to chicken breast.

Upon eating roasted armadillo, English naturalist Charles Darwin commented that they "taste and look like a duck."

the cooked armadillos were nearly identical to those found at the archaeological site. The scientists concluded that modern Argentineans cook armadillos the same way their ancestors did: fire-roasted in the shell.

The armadillo's value can be seen in thousands of years' worth of artwork made by native peoples. When the Chiriqui people of Costa Rica and Panama discovered gold and began trading with other civilizations about 1,000 years ago, they fashioned ornate jewelry. Armadillos were a common theme, and gold armadillo pendants have been collected by museums around the world, including the Yale Peabody Museum of Natural History in Connecticut. The Walters Art Museum in Baltimore is home to one of the most extensive collections of Chiriqui artifacts, including pottery shaped like armadillos. Like many cultures of **Mesoamerica** that made pottery from terra cotta (a type of baked clay), the Kuna people of Panama and the Calima people of Colombia crafted cups, pots, bowls, and **fetishes** in the shape of armadillos for use in rituals. The British Museum is now home to an armadillo-shaped ocarina, which is a type of flute. In Berlin, the Ethnological

Museum's collection of Mesoamerican artifacts includes a six-banded armadillo vase that is nearly 2,000 years old.

Even before the first human civilizations rose up in South America, small tribes of people expressed their relationship with nature by etching or painting artwork on rock faces. In 2009, an accidental discovery in southwestern Brazil revealed ancient depictions of armadillos on cave walls. Wildlife Conservation Society researchers led by biologist Dr. Alexine Keuroghlian were tracking white-lipped peccaries (wild relatives of the pig) when they stumbled upon a cave whose walls had been covered with human figures, geometric

Found among other items in ancient tombs near Colima, Mexico, were armadillo-shaped vessels from about 300 B.C.–A.D. 300.

from "THE BEGINNING OF THE ARMADILLO"

"Mother," [Painted Jaguar] said, "there are two new animals in the woods to-day, and the one that you said couldn't swim, swims, and the one that you said couldn't curl up, curls; and they've gone shares in their prickles, I think, because both of them are scaly all over, instead of one being smooth and the other very prickly; and, besides that, they are rolling round and round in circles, and I don't feel comfy."

"Son, son!" said Mother Jaguar ever so many times, graciously waving her tail, "a Hedgehog is a Hedgehog, and can't be anything but a Hedgehog; and a Tortoise is a Tortoise, and can never be anything else."

"But it isn't a Hedgehog, and it isn't a Tortoise. It's a little bit of both, and I don't know its proper name."

"Nonsense!" said Mother Jaguar. "Everything has its proper name. I should call it 'Armadillo' till I found out the real one. And I should leave it alone."

So Painted Jaguar did as he was told, especially about leaving them alone; but the curious thing is that from that day to this, O Best Beloved, no one on the banks of the turbid Amazon has ever called Stickly-Prickly and Slow-Solid anything except Armadillo. There are Hedgehogs and Tortoises in other places, of course (there are some in my garden); but the real old and clever kind, with their scales lying lippety-lappety one over the other, like pine-cone scales, that lived on the banks of the turbid Amazon in the High and Far-Off Days, are always called Armadillos, because they were so clever.

excerpt from Just So Stories,
by Rudyard Kipling (1865–1936)

shapes, and a variety of animals—including armadillos. **Anthropologists** immediately began studying the cave art, which could have been created as long ago as 10,000 years. Older rock art can be found in northeastern Brazil's Serra da Capivara National Park. Named a World Heritage Site, the secluded area is covered with rock art featuring images of humans hunting animals such as deer and armadillos. The site has been dated to 25,000 years ago. Some scientists believe the rock art is older—perhaps 36,000 years old, which would make it the oldest rock art in the Americas.

The friendly Fuleco was popular amongst Brazilians—especially with the target audience of children.

The armadillo is still such an important figure in South America that the Brazilian three-banded armadillo served as the official mascot of the 2014 FIFA World Cup soccer competition, which took place in Brazil. The mascot was named Fuleco, a combination of the Portuguese words *futebol* (football) and *ecologia* (ecology), and encouraged environmental awareness. In North America, the nine-banded armadillo has become a peculiar symbol of the American Southwest. Common souvenirs in Texas include armadillo shell baskets (with the tail curled over the shell like a handle), lampshades, and purses. Armadillos are also stuffed and dressed up with miniature cowboy hats and pistols in gun belts. Country music legend and native Texan Willie Nelson even has a stuffed armadillo. Received as a gift from a fan in 2010, "Ol' Dillo" has become the unofficial mascot of Nelson's band, appearing onstage at every concert. After more than a century of jokes, the armadillo finally got some respect from the state of Texas, which declared the armadillo its official mascot in 1981.

Perhaps because of their odd appearance, armadillos figure as quirky characters in a variety of games and other media. Mighty the Armadillo made his debut in the 1993 arcade game *SegaSonic the Hedgehog* and went on to appear in the video game *Knuckles' Chaotix* two years later. He also appeared in several Sonic the Hedgehog comic books. With his signature red shell and sneakers, the teenaged Mighty struck a deal with Mammoth Mogul, who granted him the power of super strength. Mighty can run 200 miles (322 km) per hour and roll into a tough ball resistant to weapons. Other armadillo characters appearing in video games include the robotic Armored Armadillo in *Mega Man X* and Army Dillo in *Donkey Kong 64*.

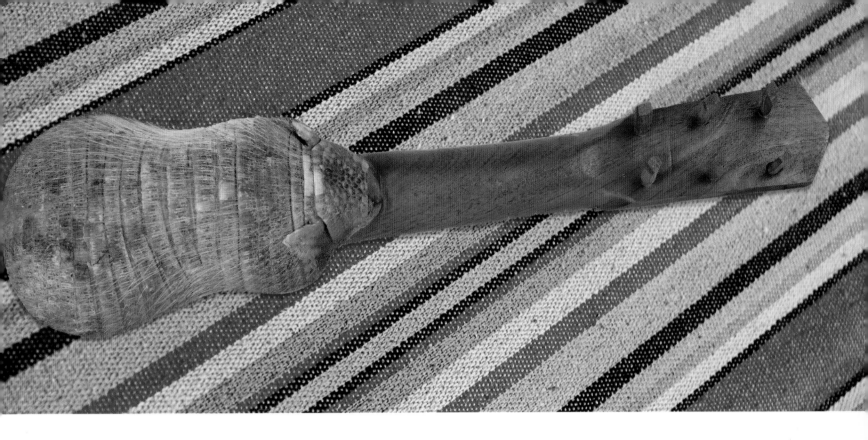

Armadillos can be found in other animated forms as well. The 2015 3D movie *El Americano* is the first animated movie coproduced by Mexican and American studios. The story involves a crazy cast of animals that are common in Mexico and the American Southwest—including a wrestling nine-banded armadillo named Trueno. Fans of Japanese anime may recall Armalady the armadillo, one of many strange animals in the 2002 anime series *Princess Tutu*. And the 2002 movie *Ice Age* features a prehistoric armadillo relative that isn't very bright. Eddie the glyptodont throws himself off a cliff, cheerfully crying out, "Look, I'm flying!" Several more sensible glyptodont characters appear in all the *Ice Age* movie sequels as well as the spin-off short film *Surviving Sid* (2008).

A traditional musical instrument of the Andes region was once made with the shell of an armadillo.

Nine-banded armadillos have adapted easily to life in Florida's humid environment.

THEY ONLY COME OUT AT NIGHT

To preserve a species, scientists must understand the animal's reproductive habits. Because researchers have never even seen the mating behavior or offspring of many armadillo species, little can be done to evaluate their status. The IUCN lists five species, including the hairy long-nosed and fairy armadillos, as lacking enough information to classify. Conservationists fear that these armadillo species could disappear before humans have the opportunity to properly study them. On the other hand, eight species appear to have healthy populations with little to threaten their existence in their natural habitats. Five others, including the Chacoan naked-tailed and the southern and northern (Llanos) long-nosed armadillo, are listed as near threatened. And three species, including the Andean hairy and giant armadillo, are listed as vulnerable. This means that if current trends in human expansion, land and water use, overhunting, and habitat destruction continue unchecked, these armadillos could face extinction.

Conservation biologist Mariella Superina, the chair of the IUCN Anteater, Sloth, and Armadillo Specialist Group, stated in 2012 that most scientists had been

Similar to their anteater relatives, armadillos possess long, sticky tongues used to pull insects from tunnels.

Giant armadillos have voracious appetites and can eat 200,000 ants in a single night.

Most armadillo species sleep for up to 16 hours a day, emerging from burrows at night to search for prey.

studying either dead armadillos or common armadillo species kept in zoos. This meant that very little in-the-field research had been conducted on armadillos. In addition, Superina reported that the few field studies conducted have yielded poor results. Brazilian biologists Kena F. M. da Silva and Raimundo Paulo Barros Henriques had only modest success in studying seven-banded armadillos in 2009. The scientists set numerous live traps in an effort to capture some of the elusive armadillos. However, because armadillos are highly alert to changes in their environment, they almost always avoid traps. Out of 9,205 trap settings, da Silva and Henriques caught only about 20 armadillos—far too few to gather significant data.

In 2002, biologist Dr. Arnaud Desbiez of the Royal Zoological Society of Scotland (RZSS) went to Brazil to study giant armadillos. It wasn't until he helped launch the Pantanal Giant Armadillo Project in 2011 that he saw his first giant armadillo. The Pantanal—the world's largest tropical wetland—covers portions of Brazil, Paraguay, and Bolivia. The Giant Armadillo Project is the first long-term, on-site study of giant armadillos, highly secretive

animals that spend 75 percent of their time underground. Using various methods, researchers hope to learn about giant armadillos and their place in the **ecosystem**.

As of 2015, the project had captured fewer than 10 live giant armadillos. Researchers attach a radio transmitter to the tail of each armadillo. This tiny device sends out a signal that allows researchers to track the armadillo's movements and activities by using an antenna and a device that emits a pinging sound. The transmitter will eventually fall off, posing no risk to the animal. Researchers follow tagged armadillos all night, mapping their movements as they travel throughout their home range.

The screaming hairy armadillo is named for the high-pitched squealing sound it makes when threatened.

Armadillos limit blood flow to the legs through a system of blood vessels called a rete mirabile (Latin for "wonderful net").

The project also uses special cameras to capture images of armadillos in the wild. Since armadillos are nocturnal, the cameras have infrared capabilities that allow images to be recorded in the dark. Each camera is remotely connected to a motion-sensing device that is placed low to the ground near armadillo burrows. When the armadillo walks past the device, the movement trips the remote camera, which snaps a series of photographs or records video. Dozens of photographs and videos of armadillos and other nocturnal animals have been taken since the project began, providing valuable data on behaviors never before witnessed.

Over the course of the study, other armadillo species have presented themselves. Researchers have captured video footage of six-banded, nine-banded, and southern naked-tailed armadillos. In addition, researchers have learned that 20-some different species of animals use armadillo burrows for shelter and search for small prey in the soft dirt around the burrows. Dr. Desbiez calls giant armadillos "ecosystem engineers" because their burrows provide shelter and safety to more than 20 other species, including lizards, anteaters, and birds. One of the Giant Armadillo Project's greatest achievements occurred in 2013, when a camera trap caught images of a mother giant armadillo leading her baby out of their burrow. The video marked the first time in history anyone had ever reported seeing a baby giant armadillo. This and other armadillo videos are available on the RZSS website at www.rzss.org.uk.

In North America, armadillo research has a very different purpose. The nine-banded armadillo is the only armadillo species that carries Hansen's disease, or leprosy. Between 500 and 800 years ago, Europeans unknowingly

The screaming hairy armadillo generates a sound of more than 118 decibels—as loud as a chainsaw.

Prior to the 1970s, the pichi's range was limited, but roads and bridges have helped it expand.

The only armadillo that **hibernates**, the pichi drops its body temperature by 40 percent during its winter sleep, from May to August.

brought the disease to South America, where nine-banded armadillos somehow contracted it. As these animals moved northward, they carried the disease with them. Researchers estimate that as many as 20 percent of armadillos in the U.S. are now carriers of leprosy. And each year, as many as 250 humans contract the disease from eating undercooked meat from infected armadillos. While leprosy is not usually fatal, it does cause serious nerve damage in humans. Contrary to popular belief, leprosy cannot be contracted by handling armadillos. One must eat the armadillo to become infected. Because armadillos carry the disease, they are perfect test subjects for researchers seeking a **vaccine** for it.

Armadillos' unique physical characteristics have also inspired human engineering. Armadillo armor provided a model for a super-tough material. Mechanical engineer Francois Barthelat of Quebec's McGill University leads a project that combines six-sided glass plates with soft rubber to form sheets of flexible but tough material. The material could be used in protective coatings, flexible electronic devices, and even improved forms of body armor. Current body armor used by police and the

military is bulky and inflexible, restricting the movement of the wearer. In addition, standard bulletproof vests can be punctured by sharp objects. Barthelat's new material is highly flexible and roughly 70 percent more puncture-resistant than current bulletproof vests.

As shy, nocturnal animals that spend most of their time underground, armadillos are difficult to study. In many wild areas, armadillos exist in stable numbers, but in places where these animals must compete for resources with humans, their numbers are low. Without people's careful efforts to address the threats to armadillo habitats, some of the most interesting species could disappear before getting the chance to reveal their secrets.

Armadillos may not rush away from people, but when they smell humans, they move in the other direction.

ANIMAL TALE: HOW ARMADILLO BECAME MUSICAL

The Highland Quechua (*KESH-wa*) of Bolivia love music, and they have created various instruments that are uniquely Bolivian. One such instrument is the *kirkinchu*, more commonly known as the *charango*. This Bolivian folk tale explains how the armadillo gave its life for the creation of the kirkinchu—whose name means "armadillo."

Armadillo lived in a burrow under a farmer's shed, and at night he would roam the forest. Armadillo loved music. He longed to join the choruses of other animals, but he had no musical talent. Some nights he would lie down on the riverbank and listen to the frogs singing to each other. He did not know the language of the frogs, but that did not matter to him. He just enjoyed the chorus. He would sigh and say to the frogs, "I wish I could make music like you."

The frogs giggled, for their songs were making fun of Armadillo. They thought he was the silliest creature they had ever seen. "Silly Armadillo wants to sing," they chimed, "but silly Armadillo has a silly voice."

Armadillo also loved to listen to the music made by the crickets. He would often stop near their home and lie in the tall grass, listening. He did not know the language of the crickets, either, but he did not mind. He only loved to hear their beautiful songs.

But the crickets knew Armadillo was listening. They made fun of him in their songs. "Silly Armadillo wants to play music," they chirped, "but silly Armadillo has no talent."

One night, Armadillo was so overcome with sadness at not being able to make music that he went to see Pachamama, the mother of the world.

Armadillo begged for a voice like the frogs' or talent like the crickets'.

"Each is made in his own way," Pachamama explained to Armadillo. "The only way for you to be musical now is to die and be remade."

"Oh," cried Armadillo, "I would not mind dying if I could become musical."

"I do not think you understand what this means," said Pachamama. "You should take some time to think before making such a big decision."

Armadillo agreed. He bid Pachamama farewell and went on his way. In the darkness, Armadillo heard the songs of the frogs and crickets. He stopped to listen, his heart breaking because he could not join in. Armadillo made up his mind. He went back to see Pachamama. "Please," he begged her, "please make me musical."

"Very well," said Pachamama, "but you must die and be remade."

"Yes, yes," said Armadillo.

Some time later, Armadillo awoke. He could not feel his body. He was now a spirit floating in the night sky. He looked down from the stars and saw the farmer sitting near his shed, where Armadillo once lived. The farmer was playing the most beautiful music that Armadillo had ever heard. And he was playing it on Armadillo's body! Armadillo had been remade as the kirkinchu. This made Armadillo very happy.

The frogs and crickets heard the music and came to listen. "Look," they cried out, "Armadillo is making music!" Now, when someone plays music on the kirkinchu, the frogs and crickets join in the songs, and Armadillo listens from the stars above and smiles.

GLOSSARY

anthropologists – scientists who study the history of humankind

archaeological – relating to the study of human history through the examination of ancient peoples and their artifacts

diurnal – active during the daytime

ecosystem – a community of organisms that live together in an environment

embryos – unborn or unhatched offspring in the early stages of development

extinct – having no living members

fetishes – objects believed by certain cultures to embody spirits or possess magical powers

fragmentation – the breaking up of an organism's habitat into scattered sections that may result in difficulty moving safely from one place to another

genetically – relating to genes, the basic physical units of heredity

gestation – the period of time it takes a baby to develop inside its mother's womb

hibernates – spends the winter in a sleeplike state in which breathing and heart rate slow down

mammals – warm-blooded animals that have a backbone and hair or fur, give birth to live young, and produce milk to feed their young

Mesoamerica – the area from central Mexico through Central America, including Belize, El Salvador, Guatemala, and Honduras

roadkill – an animal or animals killed by a vehicle on a roadway

solitary – alone, without companions

uterus – the organ in a female mammal's body where offspring develop before birth; another word for "womb"

vaccine – a substance to provide protection from a disease

venom – poison produced in an animal's body

weaned – made the young of a mammal accept food other than nursing milk

SELECTED BIBLIOGRAPHY

Klemm, W. R. *Dillos: Roadkill on Extinction Highway?* Bryan, Tex.: Benecton Press, 2007.

Loughry, W. J., and Colleen M. McDonough. *The Nine-Banded Armadillo: A Natural History*. Norman: University of Oklahoma Press, 2013.

National Geographic. "Armadillo." http://animals .nationalgeographic.com/animals/mammals/armadillo.

National Wildlife Federation. "Wildlife: Nine-Banded Armadillo." http://www.nwf.org/wildlife/wildlife-library /mammals/nine-banded-armadillo.aspx.

Royal Zoological Society of Scotland. "Giant Armadillo Project." http://www.rzss.org.uk/conservation-programmes /projects/current-projects/giant-armadillo-project.

Wainwright, Mark. *The Mammals of Costa Rica: A Natural History and Field Guide*. Ithaca, N.Y.: Cornell University Press, 2007.

Note: Every effort has been made to ensure that any websites listed above were active at the time of publication. However, because of the nature of the Internet, it is impossible to guarantee that these sites will remain active indefinitely or that their contents will not be altered.

Armadillos can do little to
avoid human interference,
so people must respect
their desire for solitude.

INDEX